Eastern Military Thought

Eastern Military Thought

Colonel Harjeet Singh (Retd)

(Established 1870)

United Service Institution of India

New Delhi (India)

Vij Books India Pvt Ltd
New Delhi (India)

Published by

Vij Books India Pvt Ltd
(Publishers, Distributors & Importers)
2/19, Ansari Road
Delhi – 110 002
Phones: 91-11-43596460, 91-11-47340674
Mob: 98110 94883
e-mail: contact@vijpublishing.com
web : www.vijbooks.in

First Published in India in 2022

Contents

Introduction

The transformation of global politics and changing patterns of authority, identities and resource distribution, in any era, are usually accompanied by anxiety and instability. Whatever the precise form it assumes, tomorrow's world is likely to be more complex and probably more unpredictable than the present. Be that as it may, war and warfare have been a constant in human history. To understand war, one has to study its philosophy, grammar and logic. The nature of war changes; its structure and actors evolve along the ages. The changing environment influences the actors, and by increasing their capabilities, actors influence the domain. Throughout history, military theorists have tried to shape old sets of rules to fit the changing conditions of their contemporary times.

Western military historians began showing concern of the East at war in the aftermath of the 9/11 events. Those attacks gave a powerful thrust to cultural determinism in war and studies started by the presumably inevitable clash of civilisations.[1] It hypothesised that the fault lines between civilisations are becoming the central lines of conflict in global politics. This further manifested in writings of Western military historians and strategists on the distinction between Western and Eastern ways of war. It suggested that both sides had their distinctive military and warring traditions, and gratuitously gave the higher ground to the West on every aspect of warfare. This requires a deeper scrutiny, analysis and understanding.

The 9/11 events took the United States (U.S.) by surprise as the first-ever attack on its 'mainland'. It caused a tendency among academia and strategists to divert attention from the U.S. failure to avert them by blaming the modus operandi of the attackers on a supposedly quintessential oriental way of war, based on deceit and cunning; and conversely sublimating the ensuing response as proceeding from a superb, frontal and unambiguous 'Western way of war' which allegedly dates back to the Greeks. It is said to surpass all other civilisations' warrior traditions, with America being its ultimate incarnation and the guardian of its 'formidable' legacy, given its unparalleled technological and military supremacy.

The Western culture of war could be characterised by seeking battle to gain a rapid decision, with emphasis on shock warfare, face-to-face combat, and a singular lethality, whereas the Eastern one is portrayed as one of deception, a penchant for indirect combat, an avoidance of close-in warfare, and a preference for stand-off weaponry and missile-oriented tactics.[2] Oriental warfare was considered different and apart from European warfare.[3]

Thus, the figure of the oriental warrior is constructed as deceitful, irrational, emotional, vengeful and capable of unruly violence. Western soldiers in contrast, represent rational individuals who operate within armies that are "made for industrial battles, decisive plots of organised force, and orchestrated manoeuvres"[4] with "rational, orderly, calculated bureaucracies with a sophisticated division of labour, high-tech weapon systems and clear lines of authority from civilian politicians."[5]

This inclination to differentiate between Western and Eastern ways of war seems to draw on past legacies, distinguishing between barbaric and civilised modes of warfare. The considered view was that savages were easily impressed by "a bold and resolute procedure", i.e., by overwhelming force, and were readily suppressed by shows of firmness.[6] The argument suggested that a society's mode of war is linked to its degree of civilisation and united cultures as diverse as ancient China, medieval Arabia, and modern Turkey, stretching from the writings of Sun Tzu through the modus operandi of modern-day Islamist insurgencies.[7]

This hypothesis emphasised the key idea that war is intrinsically cultural and claimed the existence of a separate Oriental warrior tradition, characterised mainly by "evasion, delay and indirectness".[8] It also contended that this long-standing tradition which dates back to ancient China and Persia had reappeared in a variety of forms throughout history. One example was the tactics of evasion and retreat used by the Vietcong against the U.S. in the Vietnam War:

> "If I thought Huntington's view had a defect, it was that he did not discuss what I think the crucial ingredient of any Western-Islamic conflict, their quite distinctively different ways of making war. Westerners fight face to face, in stand-up battle, and go on until one side or the other gives in. They choose the crudest weapons available, and use them with appalling violence, but observe what, to non-Westerners may well seem curious rules of honour. Orientals, by contrast, shrink from pitched battle, which they often deride as a sort of game, preferring ambush, surprise, treachery and deceit as the best way to overcome an enemy."[9]

Surprise and deceit have been a constant and universal component of war and strategy. Clausewitz, the ultimate reference of Western military thought, wrote of the universal desirability of achieving surprise in warfare.[10] Regarding deception, Machiavelli, an oft-quoted figure of European statecraft, asserted that he who overcomes the enemy by fraud is as much to be praised as he who does so by force. The very word *stratagem*, which evokes strategy, means artifice and trick, especially to outwit an enemy. Another military term, manoeuvre, means self-contradictory action that seeks to circumvent the greater strengths of the enemy and to exploit his weaknesses:

> "It is the struggle of adversarial forces that generates the logic of strategy, which is always and everywhere paradoxical, and as such is diametrically opposed to the common sense, linear logic of everyday life. Thus, we have, for example, the Roman *si vis pacem, para bellum*, if you want peace, prepare for war, or tactically, the bad road is the good road in war, because its use is unexpected—granting surprise and thus at least a brief exemption from the entire predicament of a two-sided human struggle."[11]

Western warfare history is replete with battles where military deception was decisive. They demonstrate that deception and overwhelming force are not "mutually exclusive absolutes"[12] and are not the preserve of one particular culture or civilisation. In fact, weaker belligerents, regardless of their geographical location or ethnic origin, seek, out of strategic calculation, to avoid direct exposure to the devastating attacks of a much stronger foe using disproportionate force and sophisticated weaponry. It is a human pattern of behaviour that is as old as the David and Goliath confrontation. In fact, such behaviour is much more rational than the otherwise, rather suicidal, direct clash in a context of extreme power imbalance, which runs counter to the most primordial of instincts, that of self-preservation.

Even if technological breakthroughs and sophisticated weaponry have given a military edge to Western societies, cultural differences remain the most determinant elements in winning battles and wars. After the first campaign in Afghanistan, many Western historians and strategists euphorically, and rather prematurely celebrated the rapid rout of the Taliban, which bore proof to the superior lethality of liberal democracies. The subsequent developments in both Afghanistan and Iraq and the emergence of hybrid warfare have clearly demonstrated the limits of such theories about uninterrupted Western superiority in the historical context of culturally determined ways of war. It assumes that war and warfare is simply about powerful men — mainly white men — fighting each other and/or oppressing vulnerable groups.

Military historians are now increasingly interested in the interactions between culture and war. How, for example, might a society's shared preconceptions about the nature of war influence the way their armed forces fight? If we understand the concept of culture as a set of shared beliefs, understandings, and behaviours evolved to promote success or survival in the world, then it makes sense to suggest that the especially stressful environment of war promotes its own "cultures"—and it does so at several different levels. Participants in war, whether as polities or as individuals, develop specific cultures in response to its demands. Thus, political leaders and military commanders develop systems of thought, which they deem rational, about what victory means and how one may best achieve it.

Historians regularly cite patterns in national approaches to war, dictated partly by geography, subsistence system, or political structure, but nonetheless promoting a set of intellectual approaches to the problem of winning war, which shape the dynamics of warfighting. Strategic culture forms a significant thread within military history. Scholars have gone so far as to suggest that there are "civilisational" ways of war, positing a Western way versus an Eastern way which has more than just academic interest. Modern-day analysts and political leaders make calculations of likely enemy responses based on a sometimes-shallow assessment of their opponent's strategic culture. Indeed, some of the strategic culture literature was first generated to fill this need for prediction.

The last half century has seen significant reorientations in military history. For a long time, the study of war was the prerogative of military officers, who were dealing primarily with strategy and tactics. After World War II, many historians paid greater attention to the interaction of war with societies, economics, and politics.[13] This allowed the history of war to become a well-taught academic discipline in universities, mainly in the Anglo-Saxon world.[14]

Military experiences and technologies also travelled from East to West. Within this framework, the Mongols played a pivotal role as intermediaries of cultural transfer. It is likely that the military machine of the Mongols played a prominent role in the dissemination of gunpowder throughout the Islamic world and from the East to the West (as well as throughout Western Europe).[15]

Western military studies are often dominated by the writings of Carl von Clausewitz, the Prussian author of *On War*, and Antoine Henri de Jomini, his contemporaneous Swiss counterpart and author of *The Art of War*.[16] Clausewitz is often cited for his clear pronouncements on the political nature of strategy and the importance of a holistic, systems-based approach to understanding the nature of warfare as an instrument of policy. In comparison, Jomini's concepts are essential to modern approaches to operational art, which owes its terminology largely to his writings. In many ways, the development of western political-military strategy is based on Clausewitz, while military operational planning has been based on Jomini. Modern Western military doctrine and practice have absorbed these thinkers' insights and concepts; their impact on modern Western military strategy has been monumental, by any measurement.

That acknowledged, non-Western cultures have had their own theorists, and their approaches to military strategy have ardent followings of their own. Significantly, China, India, Japan and the Islamic world each have a robust military tradition that, in part at least, reflects the thinking of a particular military theorist. In fact, the writings of these venerable civilisations predate those of Clausewitz and Jomini by centuries. Given the global nature of modern warfare, 21st-century military commanders would be well advised to familiarise themselves with these writings in this age of coalition warfare, where potential coalition partners and possible adversaries may be grounded in strategic thinking derived from major non-Western military theorists.

From China, Sun Tzu's *Art of War* is a collection of aphorisms and maxims, in thematic chapters. The text was ostensibly compiled in the 5th century BCE, and has been edited, amended, and revised by commentators and subsequent theorists - some of whom are identifiable and others unknown.[17] Kautilya's *Arthaśāstra*, in India, credited as written between 321-150 BCE, is another ancient military text (amongst aspects of statecraft and administration) that is daunting in its scope and range of subject matter. It includes a good deal of prescriptive tabular material on such non-military topics.[18] A more recent addition is Miyamoto Musashi's *The Book of Five Rings*, from Japan, which can be dated accurately to 1645 CE.[19]

These theorists, especially Sun Tzu and Kautilya, are so removed from the 21st century and so mythical in reputation that their very existence is moot. Even Musashi, a person whom one can date with reasonable precision, is a figure whose martial exploits are clouded in legend. It is not the purpose of this monograph to debate their actual historicity or determine the accuracy of the attribution of the works credited to them. For our purpose, we accept their authorship, era, and attributed works.

Accepting that as a premise, these ancient strategists present contemporary strategists and planners a cultural lens through which to view strategic thought and campaign design. When aspects of cultures are applied to strategic issues, the refraction that occurs in that culture is, by nature, an accretion of almost imperceptible and invariably local influences. It is questionable whether an outsider can ever fully appreciate the full depth and scope of a different culture unless that person has been shaped in that same crucible.

Conversely, strategic thinking is, by its nature, cross-cultural and universal in its intent. Principles of war generally come from the integration of the universal purposes of strategy. They are difficult to codify even in a stable, homogeneous culture, much less across diverse ones.[20] However, as culture reflects the approaches a people use to solve problems, attempting to grasp the cultural context of another society's actions, whether adversary or ally, is essential to designing the actions that one may take in their own context.

Chapter – 1

CHINA

Chinese strategic and military thought dates back some 5,000 years. Though Sun Tzu's *Art of War* is the best known of Chinese texts on strategy, there are other highly influential texts and traditions as well. During the Sung dynasty (960-1126 CE) scholars collected the seven most profound military classics, the apogee of Chinese military thought as written by its ancient generals. These classics are:[21]

> *Tai Gong Liu Tao* (Six Secret Teachings)

> *Sima Fa* (The Minister of War's Methods)

> *Sun Bing Fa* (Sun Bin's Art of War)

> *Wu Zi* (Teachings of Wu Qi)

> *Wei Liao Zi* (Teachings of Wei Liao)

> *Huangshi Gong Sanlue* (Three Strategies of Huang Shih-kung)

> *Tang Taizong Li Weigong Wendui* (Dialogue Between T'ang T'ai-tsung and Li Wei-kung)

Amongst these classics Sun Tzu's *Art of War* is considered primary. He is perhaps the greatest writer on military affairs who ever lived.[22] The ancient Chinese scholars believed that while imperial benevolence was the best way to avert dissension and civil unrest, the empire could not survive

9

without a strong military. Chinese emperors relied on their armies to protect them against "barbarian" invasions by violent nomadic tribesmen. Be that as it may, most Chinese rulers preferred non-military solutions to their empire's problems.

China's culture of war is ancient and highly developed. An example of this is the thousands upon thousands of terra-cotta warriors found in the tomb of Shih Huang-ti, the emperor who used fire and sword to unite China for the first time.[23] Shih Huang-ti considered *The Art of War* an essential text, and so it escaped the book burning of his reign. Liddell Hart names Sun Tzu one of the most influential military thinkers of the past: "In brief, Sun Tzu was the best short introduction to the study of warfare, and no less valuable for constant reference in extending study of the subject."[24] However, ancient Chinese military thought was unknown to Europe until the late 18th century; therefore, Western military concepts found their origins in their own history.

Sun Tzu's *Art of War*, as passed down through the ages, consists of thirteen chapters of varying length, each ostensibly focused upon a specific topic. While Chinese military scholars characterise the entire work as an organic whole, marked by the logical progression and development of themes from start to finish, obvious relationships between supposedly connected passages are frequently difficult to determine. However, the major concepts generally receive frequent, consistent treatment throughout, supporting the attribution of the book to a single figure or well-integrated school of thought.[25] The work is remarkably lucid, if compressed and sometimes enigmatic.

Little is known about Sun Tzu as a historical person. He was most likely born in the late Eastern Zhou Dynasty when the kings had become nominal figureheads, and China fragmented into over a hundred feudal states governed by competing warlords. Records from that period are understandably sparse. Sun Tzu is variously attributed as a citizen of the states of Wu and of Ch'i. However, enough details exist to ascertain that *The Art of War* probably was written during the Warring States period in China (c. 403-221 BCE).[26]

It was Sun Tzu who first made the case that war is part of politics, a discipline that must be studied and mastered. *The Art of War* is the world's oldest military treatise, yet one that remains relevant today, studied by generals, business leaders, sports coaches, and politicians as a general guide to strategy. It is also a work of moral philosophy, dealing with the rightness or wrongness of the decision to wage war, as well as the proper and moral way to conduct war - what is referred to as *casus belli* (an event used to justify starting a war) and *jus in bello* (the law that governs the way in which warfare is conducted). The structure and text of *The Art of War* is condensed and fragmented, a collection of aphorisms rather than a descriptive narrative. Such a work would be improbable outside of a long-established tradition of military art and science based on extensive battle experience.[27]

In the social and military conditions of the Warring States, intrigue, deception, diplomacy, and other political skulduggery played an important, even crucial, role in sustaining national power and husbanding military resources. In such an environment, Sun Tzu's opening comment is fully appropriate in describing the context and intent of his work: "War is a matter of vital importance to the state; the province of life or death; the road to survival or ruin. It is mandatory that it be thoroughly studied."[28]

Sun Tzu wrote for a time when the state's capability to make war was limited. Standing armies were expensive and time-consuming to recruit and maintain. The ancient Chinese state's capacity to make war was dependent on the season. Raising an army took time. Thus, "supreme excellence consists in breaking the enemy's resistance without fighting." Making war too expensive for the enemy is best; worst of all possibilities is siege warfare. However, it is a universal truth of warfare that if you deprive the enemy of the capacity to make war, victory will follow.

Just as Sun Tzu's writing, with its references to chariots and signal fires, cannot be separated from its historical context, neither can it be separated from its unique social and military context. For example, his question as to "which of the two sovereigns is imbued with the Moral Law?" To Sun Tzu, uprightness and good generalship are inseparable. Moral weakness - anger, impatience, cowardice, even oversolicitousness of the welfare of one's troops - will lead to military weakness. To Sun Tzu, the ideal general should be a great planner: "If you know the enemy and know yourself, you need not fear the result of a hundred battles. If you know yourself but not the enemy, for every victory gained you will also suffer a defeat. If you know neither the enemy nor yourself, you will succumb in every battle."[29] Sun Tzu placed prime emphasis on diplomacy and informational uses of power: "Generally in war the best policy is to take a state intact; to ruin it is inferior to this".[30]

Furthermore, "indirect tactics, efficiently applied, are inexhaustible as Heaven and Earth, unending as the flow of rivers and streams; like the sun and moon, they end but to begin anew; like the four seasons, they pass away to return once more." By comprehending the causes and nature of these changes, the general can successfully compete on the battlefield. The axioms of the *Tao* - the laws of the universe itself - are to be wielded to gain power over one's foes and to ensure the well-being of the human, political world. *The Art of War* combined two of the three main streams of ancient

Chinese philosophy. It is a work not only of military strategy but of supreme psychological insight. It gives not only the means by which to prevail in a conflict but also by which to live one's life.

Sun Tzu's era was one of restrained, limited warfare. Pitched, decisive engagements were to be avoided at all costs and undertaken only when no other recourse was feasible. No commander should embark on military action without thorough intelligence gathering, detailed analysis of one's own and the enemy's capabilities and resources, and precise planning. Deception, manoeuvre, and manipulation were a commander's principle tools: "Now war is based on deception. Move when it is advantageous and create changes in the situation by dispersal and concentration of forces."[31]

In general, Sun Tzu's conceptual approach was one of indirect, even circuitous, lines of operation: "Nothing is more difficult than the manoeuvre. What is difficult about manoeuvre is to make the devious route the most direct and to turn misfortune to advantage".[32] Sun Tzu advocated manoeuvre and indirect methods of action, exploiting intelligence, resource depletion, and deception. He urged the avoidance of battle until the commander determined that conditions were auspicious. It is easy to read into Sun Tzu's writings one's own predilections.[33] It is also easy to follow his advice selectively. Hence, Sun Tzu's maxims are often quoted in isolation and not used in a sophisticated, cohesive way when applied to strategy development and campaign design. Sun Tzu did not define strategy, but he offered pointers on its practice. Also, at times, Sun Tzu can be straightforward and simplistic: "Victory is the main object of war".

Sun Tzu advocated deception and winning without fighting: "For to win one hundred victories in one hundred battles is not the acme of skill. To subdue the enemy without fighting is the acme of skill." Sun Tzu advocated winning by manoeuvre or by psychologically dislocating the opponent and explained how to manoeuvre and fight: "If I am able to determine the enemy's dispositions while at the same time, I conceal my own then I can concentrate and he must divide. And if I concentrate while he divides, I can use my entire strength to attack a fraction of his."

Sun Tzu opined that the defence was the stronger form of warfare but that offensive action was necessary for victory: "Invincibility lies in the defence; the possibility of victory in the attack.... One defends when his strength is inadequate; he attacks when it is abundant." He sometimes did incomplete analysis and thus provided advice that might be wrong depending on the circumstances. For example, "To be certain to take what you attack is to attack a place the enemy does not protect", i.e., attack where the enemy does not expect it. The problem is that there is almost always a reason why the enemy does not defend a place, and it usually has to do with the limited value of that place. However, the line after the original quote changes the meaning of the entire passage: "To be certain to hold what you defend is to defend a place the enemy does not attack." It implies chance and uncertainty in war and the only certain way to take a place is if the enemy is not there. Sun Tzu, as the advocate of deception, surprise, intelligence, and manoeuvre to win without fighting, is mandatory reading for the strategist.

Sun Tzu provides basic tools for strategists at all levels to address the complexities in today's world of uncertainty, where conventional and indirect warfare tactics and techniques are required. Specifically, he brings awareness to the significance of strategy as it applies to waging war, to the concept of battle avoidance, and to the need for both military and diplomatic involvement to achieve victory. He provides a very flexible approach to address the complexities surrounding the current strategic environment that involves uncertainty, terrorism, and both irregular and asymmetrical warfare.

Sun Tzu's work has been widely influential even in the present era. Mao Zedong, the Chinese Communist leader, was himself a military theorist whose book on guerrilla warfare was inspired by *The Art of War*. Mao credited the defeat of both the Japanese invasion of China and Chiang Kai-shek's Nationalist forces to ideas and theories he had learned from Sun Tzu. The Vietnamese general Vo Nguyen Giap, during the Vietnam War, was likewise inspired by *The Art of War*, and, indeed, the Vietnamese resistance to Japanese, French, and American occupiers can be seen as an application of Sun Tzu's principles.

We can even see China's recent foreign policy as following the principles of *The Art of War*. Modern China views Sun Tzu's classic work as part of its national patrimony, part of a cultural, if not military, expansion. Whether on the battlefield or in the boardroom, there seems to be something in the Sun Tzu mystique for everyone.

Sun Tzu's theories are as valid and necessary today as they were hundreds of years ago when he wrote about strategy. Though he did not invent the principles, he observed them, used them in accordance with Chinese history, and then presented them in a way that made sense to his followers and continues to make sense to leaders and strategists today.[34] His war theories are not prescriptive in nature but provide strategic planners, political leaders, and commanders a multitude of ideas and perspectives to consider when making difficult decisions. In today's strategic environment, rather than planning for large-scale military operations, or even small wars limited to specific nation-states, strategic planners should develop strategies to tackle unconventional threats from both state and non-state actors.

Coming to recent times, a book written in 1999[35], is a discussion of modern warfare strategy and provides a somewhat different perspective from a Chinese viewpoint. It expounds that technology precedes its best employment in warfare and that military forces now must consider non-military actions if they are to be effective. There is considerable Chinese military philosophy discussed, including the *Thirty-Six Stratagems*.[36] The authors argue that modern war has evolved past using only armed forces to compel the enemy to submit to one's will, into using all military and non-military means to coerce an enemy to capitulate to a state's political objectives. According to their analysis, in the modern, highly competitive, globalised world, the roles of soldiers and civilians has been fundamentally erased because the equivalent of war among states in the modern world would now be ongoing continuously and everywhere. Another authoritative and influential publication is "*The Science of Military Strategy*" published by the Academy of Military Sciences of the People's Liberation Army of China 2001.[37]

Chapter – 2

INDIA

There is a great eclecticism in Indian philosophical traditions, which is a source of Indian civilisational strength.[38] India, as a nation-state, has a long civilisational history and experience of complex cultural exchanges that has contributed to the development of its national identity and behaviour, including the ideational and material (geographical) conceptualisation of the state. India's tradition of realist strategic thought is probably the oldest in the world. It was propounded by the strategist Kautilya, also known as Chanakya and Vishnugupta, who wrote the *Arthaśāstra*. The text contains 15 *adhikaranas* or books. Variously translated as "science of politics" or "treatise on polity", it is acknowledged by Indian scholars as the most important ancient Indian text on strategy. It is still an inspiration to modern Indian strategic and military thought. Some scholars challenge the date of Kautilya's work but none place it later than 150 CE.[39] The *Arthaśāstra*, like many of the classic Chinese texts, is a complex and subtle work, and as such is vulnerable to selective reading and interpretation. Moreover, it does not form the whole of Indian strategic tradition. While it emphasises both political flexibility and military mobility, an older tradition represented by another Indian classic text, the *Mahabharata*, emphasises annihilation of the enemy through systematic attrition.[40]

Chandragupta Maurya was the first ruler to unify most

of the Indian subcontinent in a single empire. He turned back Alexander the Great's successors, defeated the Nanda kings, and established an effective imperial rule. Kautilya was the architect of Chandragupta's rise. The *Arthaśāstra* is a comprehensive record of actions and advice on governing a vast empire, to include military strategy.[41] "Kautilya did not say to himself, 'Prepare for war, but hope for peace;' but instead, 'Prepare for war, and plan for conquest.'"[42] The *Arthaśāstra* is firmly predicated on two seemingly divergent strands – *artha* and *dharma*, the former alluding to material well-being and the latter to spiritual good.

Kautilya enunciated many military strategies in the *Arthaśāstra* but does not seem to have made much distinction between military strategy and that of statecraft. He believed that warfare is an extension and an integral part of statecraft.[43] He has covered an array of strategies over a vast canvas from actual fighting and planning, to training and deceit. Power, according to the *Arthaśāstra*, is the object of interstate relations, and "dissension and force" are the natural state of international relations. Power is relative and must be maximised both in absolute and relative terms, for survival and success.

The teachings in the *Arthaśāstra* include the pursuit of power through realpolitik, the use of offensive force, deception, treachery, assassination, and chicanery, and the view that conquest and the establishment of hegemony is the appropriate policy of the "good" leader. These teachings are the equal of any of the lessons in Sun Tzu's *Art of War* or any other Chinese text on strategy.

Kautilya averred that 'one either conquers or suffers conquest'. As a means to that end, he advocated making treaties while planning to break them, as well as recommending the use of spies and secret agents to assassinate enemy leaders.

On a first reading, there is little in the core text of Indian strategic thought that might clearly differentiate it from a *realpolitik* Chinese strategic culture.[44] This suggests the tendency of many Western analysts to engage in selective reading and citation of these works. The *Arthaśāstra* also has subtle and overt warnings about the dangers of war and the need for prosperity, good governance, and legitimate rule to maintain power.

Perhaps the most commonly cited idea from Kautilya is the concept of *mandalas*, or circles. Statecraft was a key factor in the march of conquest. Kautilya framed the would-be conqueror's (*vijigishu's*) problem as a *mandala*, a finely patterned ring of concentric circles. The *vijigishu* himself was at the centre. Those closer in the circle, on the borders of the state, will be enemies plotting his destruction. Next to that enemy was that enemy's enemy, and the enemy of one's enemy is a friend. Of course, once the extant enemy was disposed of, the problem was reframed because the former ally became a probable enemy. In this ever-threatening situation, peace was preferable to war only insofar as it bought time to recover from a weak position. It was a temporary expedient, and conquest should resume as soon as it is practical, whether by open warfare, pre-emptive surprise strikes, or secret sabotage.[45]

This discussion of natural enemies and natural allies has led some to interpret Kautilya's work as consistent with balance-of-power politics (or defensive realism). However, Kautilya's idea of concentric circles is not meant to be one of fixed geographic relationships. Rather, *mandalas* apply to relationships of power, influence, and interest, not only geographic proximity. Relationships are not so fixed that all border states must be enemies, although Kautilya believed that bordering states were more likely to be enemies or objects of conquest than not. Kautilya explicitly advocates conquest and holds the notion that the best leader is a "conqueror" who actively seeks to maximise power at all times, and who also constantly prepares for war either actively or passively.[46] This assumption is Clausewitzian strategy turned on its head — instead of all warfare being an instrument of policy, all policy is a means to prosecute war.

Kautilya also notes that war is dangerous and uncertain, and that if there is no prospect of one's decline relative to an enemy, then peace (while continuing to maximise prosperity and the fruits of recent conquest) is preferable to war.[47] Furthermore, generating and sustaining wealth and political legitimacy are also critical.[48] Kautilya was also deeply concerned with the moral quality of leaders, the welfare of the people, justice, and the legitimacy of the regime. In his view, justice and legitimacy in foreign policy, as well as military prowess, were necessary for a leader's success.[49]

Kautilya underscored the importance of dynamism in the growth of a state. To him passivity was improper and the objective of a State was power not just to control outward behaviour but also the thoughts of one's subjects and one's adversaries.[50] He outlined eight precepts that governed the general power of a state:

➤ Every nation acts to maximise power and self-interest.

➤ Moral principles have little or no force in actions amongst nations.

➤ Alliances are a function of mutuality.

➤ War and peace are considered solely from the perspective of what advantages they provide to the instigator.

➤ The '*mandala*' premise of foreign policy provides the basis of strategic planning of alliances and a general theory of international relations.

> Diplomacy of any nature is a subtle act of war in contrast to the Clausewitzian view of war being a continuation of polity.

> Three types of warfare are upheld, the first is *dharmayuddha* (ethical warfare), the second is *kutayuddha* (devious warfare); and lastly *tusnimyuddha* (war that is waged through silence and subterfuge).

> Seeking justice is the last desperate resort of the weak.

The *Arthaśāstra* attaches great significance to espionage and intelligence, not only about the enemy but citizen attitudes towards power. Kautilya wrote that a state could be endangered by four types of threats and challenges - internal, external, externally-supported internal and internally-supported external. He emphasised that of these four types, internal threats should be indispensably dealt with through sufficient and immediate attention. As a matter of fact, internal troubles, including revolts, rebellions, sabotages, subversions and so on, like the fear of the lurking snake, are far more serious and harmful than external threats and challenges. The most dangerous enemy is the enemy within. Kautilyan assertions on internal security and his views on a well-crafted grand strategy for the management of internal security affairs have great value for India in the changing domestic, regional and global scenarios of the 21st century.[51]

Kautilya accepted as a starting point that insecurity and instability are the dominant characteristics of the Indian environment.[52] The *Arthaśāstra* was the embodiment of ruthless realism, based on bold, pitiless action. Its reliance on duplicity was not artful subterfuge, but deliberate deception and bloody assassination. The ultimate aim remained conquest, pure and simple.[53] As Max Weber noted about the *Arthaśāstra*, "Compared to it, Machiavelli's *The Prince* is harmless."[54]

With the fundamental aim of national strategy established as conquest, Kautilya determined that all elements of power be directed at that end. In Kautilya's cynical and suspicious mind, the *vijigishu* (would-be conqueror) faced a challenging world of anarchy, fierce self-interest on the part of absolutely everyone, and deadly, immediate risk at home and abroad. Thus, for the *vijigishu* to survive, much less succeed, he must use every means at his disposal to gain and cement power. In such a context, a ruler must promote the welfare of the people, as the people are the source of his wealth, and wealth makes it possible to finance more conquests. Conquest, in turn, enlarges his domains and brings more subjects under his control, and the cycle can be repeated until there is nothing left to conquer.[55] Only then can real peace be obtained.

Nothing, then, was beneath a potentate's attention. Internal administration of the kingdom was as important as foreign relations, since the resources to conduct conquest must first be controlled and developed. Hence, *The Arthaśāstra* covered subjects as diverse as how to manage forests (forests harbour elephants, and elephants are useful for war), how Indian society functioned, income from crown property, types and purposes of marriages, how to plan a campaign, and how to treat a subjugated population. *The Arthaśāstra* is one of the earliest and most complete treatments of holistic strategic-level leadership in existence. It is also one of the most single-minded works of its kind. Every resource, every element of national power, every waking moment of a ruler's days, was to be spent with one intent — hegemonic conquest.

Does the *Arthaśāstra* represent current 21st-century thinking of leaders on the Indian subcontinent? Some authors believe Kautilya's counsel resonates even today with Indian national leaders, as it did for Chandragupta. Indeed, the Indian policy of nonalignment was directly Kautilyan—a means of enhancing security by a low-risk strategy of playing one superpower off against another until India could gain sufficient strength to protect its own security. India's current negotiating strategies on nuclear deterrence, weapons procurement, and international trade issues reflect both Kautilyan trends and India's 21st-century self-perception of its role as an emerging world power.[56] While the *Arthaśāstra* is no magical tome that offers a full explanation of Indian culture, it sets forth traditions and background that offer helpful insights into Indian strategic policies and actions even today.

Chapter – 3

JAPAN

The legend of the imperial house of Japan emerged from two stages of armed conquest. The first stage involved the Japanese domination and destruction of other races of people inhabiting the islands that were to become Japan. The second stage, which was partially concurrent with the first, was marked by the ascendancy of some Japanese clans over others. As the early Japanese grew in numbers and expanded their territories, they subjugated or annihilated the minority races, and also fought among themselves.[57]

The gradual separation of a cultural aristocracy from a martial aristocracy advanced after the capital of Japan was established in Heian, the ancient city of Kyoto, at the end of the 8th century. Leading families of powerful clans with extensive land holdings gathered in the capital and developed an urban culture. Meanwhile, frontier warrior families continued to expand territories, while provincial warrior families administered and policed the extensive holdings of the court nobles.[58] While an imperial state and central bureaucracy was established, the Japanese warrior elites retained their importance in society as governors of territories and administrators of lands and serfs held by absentee landlords. They also continued to provide the military underpinning of the entire aristocracy, as well as of the various territories and clans.

By 1100 CE, most of Japan outside of the Kyoto area

was under local military control, and the 12th century saw virtually constant civil war. In 1185 CE, the most powerful of the warrior clans established a centralised military government, the first of three such regimes to dominate Japanese society, politics, and culture for centuries to come.

The strong military presence marking internal Japanese history has imprinted certain elements of the warrior ethos onto important areas of Japanese thought and society, well beyond the context of the original art of war. For hundreds of years the *samurai* not only were masters of the political fate of the nation, but were considered the leaders of the popular conscience. The morale and spirit of the warrior was as important to their influence on society as was their material power. By the end of the 12th century, a *Shogun* or Generalissimo, was officially recognised and a military para-government was established with its own capital in eastern Japan. Over the following centuries, certain aspects of Zen and neo-Confucianism were espoused by the *samurai*, influencing the development of *Bushido* (the way of warriors), a Japanese collective term for the many codes of honour and ideals that dictated the *samurai* way of life, loosely analogous to the European concept of chivalry.[59] The "way" originates from the *samurai* moral values, most commonly stressing sincerity, frugality, loyalty, martial arts mastery, and honour until death.

Near the end of the 13th century, the Mongol rulers of China launched two attempts to invade Japan. The Japanese warriors fought off one invasion fleet. The other fleet was destroyed by storm winds, said to be a *kamikaze*, or "divine wind," believed to protect the sacred land of Japan. These events left a deep impression on the minds of the *samurai*, but they also disrupted the military order. In feudal Japan the traditional reward for victory in war was the land conquered; but the defeat of the Mongols did not produce any new territory with which to reward the deeds of the Japanese warriors.[60]

The resulting disgruntlement exacerbated the frictions inherent in the military feudal system, ultimately resulting in the toppling of the reigning dynasty of *Shoguns* in the 14th century. It was replaced by a new Shogunate, established in the imperial capital of Kyoto by another *samurai* clan and its allies. The weaknesses of the feudal lords and the ambitions of the vassals fuelled generations of warfare among the various ranks of *samurai*. The last part of the 15th century and most of the 16th century saw virtually continuous civil war. Japanese historians describe the life of warriors in those times with the phrase *ge koku jo*, ("those below overcome those above)", as long-established houses and alliances of warrior chieftains were attacked and overthrown by *samurai* from the lower ranks of the military classes. This period is known as the era of the Warring States and, in the course of prolonged warfare and military rule, the Japanese had developed what was considered the best sword craft in Asia and exported enormous quantities of fine steel blades to Ming-dynasty China, itself embroiled in civil war. It was near the end of the era of Warring States that Europeans first came to Japan, when both they and the Japanese were at new thresholds in their histories.[61]

Musashi Miyamoto (1584-1645) was a famous Japanese *samurai* and artist of the early Tokugawa period. A masterless *ronin*, he made his reputation in over sixty duels between the age of 13 and 29, and thereafter made a living teaching swordsmanship. He is credited with inventing the *nitoryu* technique of fighting with two swords. Nerveless and with the reflexes of a scorpion, he ceased using swords towards the end of his duelling career and still killed his opponents with whatever came to hand. It is said that he never combed his hair, never took a bath, and never married. His book *Go rin no Sho* (Book of Five Rings)[62] is a treatise on the art of war which focuses on *kenjutsu* (techniques for Japanese fencing) and *heihō no michi* (The Way of Combat). These two notions appear specific to Japanese culture.

In 1643, Musashi retired to a cave on Kyushu Island and completed *The Book of Five Rings* shortly before his death there in 1645. It contains the distillation of his combat experience. A recurrent phrase is: 'this should be given careful and thorough consideration.' He introduces the subject of the art of war as one among the various traditional ways of Japanese culture, to be studied and practiced by political leaders as well as by professional warriors.

Musashi regarded the way of the warrior as a special calling and mastery depended in great measure on the affinity of the practitioner with the *Dao* (way). He compares the art of war with other arts as a specialisation demanding its own characteristic inclination. People practice the ways to which they are inclined, developing individual preferences. Buddhism is a way of helping people, Confucianism is a way of civilisation, healing is a way of curing illnesses. Poets teach the way of poetry, others take to the ways of fortune telling, archery, and various other arts and crafts. Few people like the art of war.

Musashi emphasised a balanced combination of practical learning in both cultural and martial arts: "First of all," he wrote, "the way of warriors means, familiarity with both cultural and martial arts."[63] Training of this class of men was considered to be one of the most important tasks of the culture.

One of the characteristics of the warrior's way that seems to distinguish it from the way of culture is the ever-presence of death. It is commonly said that one reason warriors liked Zen Buddhism was because it taught them to face death with equanimity. Musashi, himself deeply interested in Zen, rejects this reasoning:

> "People usually assume that all warriors think about is getting used to the imminent possibility of death. As far as the process of death is concerned, warriors are not the only ones who die. All classes of people know their duty, are ashamed to neglect it, and realise that death is inevitable. There is no difference among social groups in this respect."[64]

In contrast to Sun Tzu's aphoristic approach to strategic planning and to Kautilya's broad, whole-of-monarchy nesting of all elements of national power, Miyamoto Musashi's "two swords" approach is directly operational and focused on direct approaches to combat operations. He most closely reflects Clausewitz's emphasis on centre of gravity.

Compared to the writings of Sun Tzu and Kautilya, *The Book of Five Rings* is far less accessible. It was, foremost, not so much a book of strategy as guidance on how to think strategically. Musashi wrote as if he were crafting a fencing manual, but his broad conceptual intent was to create a strategic treatise. "The principles of strategy are written down here in terms of single combat, but you must think broadly so that you attain an understanding for ten-thousand-a-side battles."[65] In strategy it is important to see distant things as if they were close and to take a distanced view of close things. Therefore, know the enemy's sword and not to be distracted by insignificant movements of his sword. The gaze is the same for single combat and for large-scale combat.

The Book of Five Rings became widely available in English in 1974, making Musashi a relative newcomer to Western students of strategic art.[66] Musashi's strategic advice emphasised directness and thoroughness. In contrast to Sun Tzu, he advocated no flourishes or deceptive manoeuvring, teaching instead that success depends on a clear focus on the objective of defeating the enemy:

> "The primary thing when you take a sword in your hands is your intention to cut the enemy, whatever the means. Whenever you parry, hit, spring, strike, or touch the enemy's cutting sword, you must cut the enemy in the same movement. It is essential to attain this. If you think only of hitting, springing, striking, or touching the enemy, you will not be able actually to cut him. More than anything, you must be thinking of carrying your movement through to cutting him. You must thoroughly research this."[67]

Whatever stance one takes, or whatever strategic ends, ways, and means one considers, Musashi advocated an objective-driven, no-nonsense attitude: "Think only of cutting."[68] Like Kautilya, Musashi was committed to a holistic approach to military strategy. In his fencing allegory, he portrayed this as the proper use of two swords. The samurai of Musashi's time carried two swords, a long sword (*katana*) generally wielded only outdoors and a shorter companion sword (*tanto* or *wazikashi*) carried at all times. Musashi called his approach *Ichi Ryu Ni To,* or "One School, Two Swords". By this, he did not mean always fighting with both swords at the same time but rather using all resources at one's disposal. "This is a truth: when you sacrifice your life, you must make fullest use of your weaponry."[69] He elaborated: "According to this Ichi school, you can win with a long weapon, and yet you can also win with a short weapon. In short, the Way of the Ichi school is the spirit of winning, whatever the weapon and whatever its size."[70]

Musashi, pointed out the importance of a holistic mindset after explaining how to best employ various weapons. What he advocated strategically was judicious balancing of ends, ways, and means when choosing a course of action.

"In large scale strategy, the superior man will manage many subordinates dexterously, bear himself correctly, govern the country and foster the people, thus preserving the ruler's discipline."[71] However, no real strategist should ever lose sight of his ultimate objective, which is to win, advance oneself, and gain honour.[72]

Musashi's writings stand in sharp contrast to Sun Tzu's *Art of War*. Sun Tzu advocated skilful battlefield manoeuvres, but Musashi saw deception and manoeuvre as a far-less-efficient means to the end than a single-minded, powerful thrust at the heart. "Do nothing which is of no use," he cautioned.[73] Once defeated, an enemy must not be offered respite, but crushed. "If we crush lightly, he may recover. The primary thing is to not let him recover his position even a little."[74]

Musashi's exploits and writings became foundational to a tradition of samurai honour - *Bushido,* which is deeply ingrained in Japanese culture and finds expression there even today across Japanese society.

Another important text on conflict and strategy emerging from the Japanese warrior culture is *The Book of Family Traditions on the Art of War*, written in 1632 by Yagyu Munenori, victorious warrior, mentor of the Shogun, and head of the Secret Service and contemporary of Musashi Miyamoto. The book consists of three main scrolls, entitled "The Killing Sword"; "The Life-Giving Sword"; and "No Sword". These are Zen Buddhist terms adapted to both wartime and peacetime principles of the *samurai*. The killing sword represents the use of force to quell disorder and eliminate violence. The life-giving sword represents the preparedness to perceive impending problems and forestall them. "No sword" represents the capacity to make full use of the resources of the environment.[75]

Chapter – 4

THE ISLAMIC WORLD

In general, little attention has been paid to the relation between the theory and the practice of war in the Islamic milieu. Narrative sources rarely provide explicit information about the actual strategies, tactics and fighting methods used in the battles. Muslim armies used various tactics on the battlefield, including feigned retreat, using archers to break the unity of the enemy groups, suddenly opening their ranks when an enemy charge was received and then closing up again and surrounding him, and charging in linear or in cohesive units, among others. The Mongols' influence on the evolution of military tactics and fighting weapons is relevant. The driving force behind them was the increased military activity in the Near East, which was widely assumed from the late 11th century by new groups coming from the East as well as from the West (e.g., Turks, Kurds, Franks and Mongols), who set up a slow but definitive militarisation of the region. The armies of the Middle East and Persia ruled the region from the pre-Islam period until the fall of the Ottoman Empire in 1918. However, Islamist terrorism is seen as one of the biggest threats to international security faced today.

It is relevant to study the subject from the time of the Prophet Muhammad and the battles he fought and those that arose subsequently. Muhammad's importance as a commander is second only to his role as a prophet. Directly or indirectly, he is supposed to have participated in no fewer than thirty-seven battles.[76] During the first twelve years of his mission in Mecca, the Muslims had neither been proclaimed an *Ummah* [77] nor had they been granted permission to take recourse to war. After their migration to Medina, a divine revelation declared them an *Ummah* and assigned them the new *Ka'aba* in Mecca, replacing the one in Jerusalem. Soon after their proclamation as an *Ummah*, the Faithful were commanded to take up arms against the Pagans.[78]

> "The universalism of Islam, in its all-embracing creed, is imposed on the believers as a continuous process of warfare, psychological and political, if not strictly military. . . . The *Jihad*, accordingly, may be stated as a doctrine of a permanent state of war, not continuous fighting."[79]

The mission assigned to the *Ummah* emphasised its moderation, justice, righteousness, practicality and universality. It laid the foundations of the political, social, economic and military philosophies of the Muslims, and formed the basis of policy and strategy. It also set in train a chain of divine revelations pertaining to state policy. As a part of its philosophy of war, the *Quran* gave the Muslims the causes and object of war; its nature, characteristics, dimensions and ethics. It also spelt out its concept of military strategy and laid down its own distinctive rules and principles for the conduct of wars.[80] Muhammad gave the people of the Middle East a religion that would unite and motivate them to conquer all of North Africa, Persia, and much of Eastern Europe.

The Quranic Concept of War, by Brigadier S.K. Malik of the Pakistani Army provides an insight to Islamic thought on war. The *Quran* is presumed to be the revealed word of God as spoken through his chosen prophet, Muhammad.

According to Malik, the *Quran* places warfighting doctrine and its theory in a much different category than western thinkers are accustomed to, because it is not a theory of war derived by man, but of God. It is God's warfighting principles and commandments revealed. Malik attempts to distil God's doctrine for war through examples of the Prophet. In the Islamic context, discussion of war is at the level of revealed truth and example, thus above theory.

The preface of *The Quranic Concept of War* by Allah Bukhsh K. Brohi, a former Pakistani ambassador to India, offers important insights into Malik's exposition. His short introductory essay preceding the text lays the foundation for the book. Malik places Quranic warfare in an academic context relative to that used by western theorists. He analyses the causes and objects of war, as well as war's nature and dimensions. He then turns to the ethics and strategy of warfare. Finally, he reviews the exercise of Quranic warfare based on the examples of the Prophet Mohammed's military campaigns and concludes with summary observations.

Zia-ul-Haq (1924-88), a former President of Pakistan and Pakistani Army Chief of Staff, in his Foreword for the book focuses on the concept of *jihad* within Islam, explaining it is not simply the domain of the military: i.e., it is not the exclusive domain of the professional soldier, nor is it restricted to the application of military force alone. His endorsement of the book established Malik's views on *jihad* as national policy. A study of *The Quranic Concept of War* is indispensable to understand the religious nature of *jihad* and implications of this doctrine for non-Muslims.

Malik argues that the nature and dimension of war is the greatest single characteristic of Quranic warfare and distinguishes it from all other doctrines. He acknowledges Clausewitz's contribution to the understanding of warfare in its moral and spiritual context. Reiterating that Muslims are required to wage war with the spirit of religious duty and obligation, Malik makes it clear that in return for fighting in the way of Allah, divine, angelic assistance will be rendered to *jihad* warriors and armies.

Malik uses examples to demonstrate that Allah will strike "terror into the hearts of Unbelievers."[81] He then explicates on the role of terror in warfare: "when God wishes to impose His will on his enemies, He chooses to do so by casting terror into their hearts."[82] "The Quranic military strategy thus enjoins us to prepare ourselves for war to the utmost in order to strike terror into the hearts of the enemies, known or hidden, while guarding ourselves from being terror-stricken by the enemy."[83] Terror is an effect; the end-state.

The contemporary relevance of *The Quranic Concept of War* is indicated by the discovery by U.S. military officials of summaries of this book published in various languages on captured and killed *jihadi* insurgents in Afghanistan. This is hardly a surprising development as Malik finds within the Quran a doctrine of aggressively escalating and constant *jihad* against non-Muslims and the religious justification of terrorism as a means to achieving the dominance of Islam around the world.

'*Jihad*', in the Quranic concept, demands the preparation and application of total national power and the military is one of its elements. As a component of the total strategy, the military strategy aims at striking terror into the hearts of the enemy from the preparatory stage of war while providing effective safeguards against being terror-stricken by the enemy. Under ideal conditions, *Jihad* can produce a direct decision and force its will upon the enemy. Where that does not happen, military strategy should take over and aim at producing the decision from the preparation stage. Should that chance be missed, terror should be struck into the enemy during the actual fighting. At all stages, however, military strategy operates as an integral part of the total strategy and not independent of it; then and then alone can it attain its designated objective.[84]

"The ability to strike terror into the enemy or to withstand the enemy attempts to terrorise us are ultimately linked with the strength of our Faith. Practised in their totality, the Quranic dimensions of war provide complete protection to the Muslim armies against any psychological breakdown. On the contrary, weaknesses in our Faith offer inroads to the enemy to launch successful psychological attacks against us. It is on the strength of our Faith, and the weakness of that of our adversary, that we can initiate plans and actions calculated to strike terror into the hearts of our adversaries."[85]

"Divine in its basic conception but human in its evolution and application, the Quranic philosophy of war consists of both constant and variable factors. The main strength of this philosophy lies in its 'constants' which, in turn, provide direction and guidance for the evolution and application of the 'variables'. An inherent lacuna in modern military thought is that it has few, if any, constants to base its theory and philosophy upon. Even the principles of war, the very essence of modern military thought, suffer from lack of constancy. Within the confines of its constants, the Quranic philosophy can absorb a great deal of the variables of the modern philosophies on war."[86]

"The only constant and immutable factor in war is the human factor; and the Quranic constants are built around it. The Quranic philosophy of war bestows upon each fighting man, leader or soldier, so firm and dominating a personality as to acquire, absorb and apply all knowledge of war effectively. It trains and prepares the man, physically, mentally and spiritually, to withstand all crises or contingencies in war. The Book wants knowledge and the human personality to flourish hand in hand; it thus strikes a happy and harmonious balance between both. The military campaigns undertaken or initiated by the Holy Prophet (peace be upon him) are 'institutions' for learning the Quranic art of war."[87]

Accordingly, Arabs resorted to their traditional methods on 11 September 2001, "appearing suddenly, out of empty space like their desert raider ancestors, assaulted the heartlands of Western power in a terrifying surprise raid and did appalling damage".[88] Hence, the most efficient way to defeat the Islamic mind, which is bent on surprise, is to apply overwhelming force by launching massive retaliation and persisting relentlessly until "the raiders have either been eliminated or so cowed by the violence".[89]

The extent and reach of Malik's thesis cannot be confirmed in the Islamic world, neither can it be discounted. Though controversial, his citations are accurately drawn from Islamic sources and consistent with classical Islamic jurisprudence.[90] When it comes to warfighting, military minds tend to focus on the combat power aspects of warfare; the tangibles of terrain, enemy, weather, leadership, and troops; and quantifiable aspects such as the ratio of forces. The study of ideology or philosophy in warfare is more cerebral than physical and not action oriented. Perhaps it is time correlate 'ideas' in the equation.

SUMMATION

It is logical to link Chandragupta's rise with Kautilya's advice, but it is difficult to tie Napoleon's operational art to Sun Tzu's maxims. Relating modern strategy to *The Book of Five Rings* is also problematic. The methodology of Eastern writings makes them prone to reinterpretation and misapplication by modern strategists and planners, who often advocate their own convictions by reference to these military philosophers.[91] Still, there are recognisable influences, and even a cursory grasp of the key essential orientation of these works can have some bearing on the way later great captains put in practice their own approaches to warfare.

Eastern military thoughts are bounded by culture and were written in differing historical contexts. The disparity in their writings makes them hard to link together in a coherent way to Western military thought. As a matter of fact, while Sun Tzu, Kautilya, Musashi and *The Quranic Concept of War* may appear on many recommended reading lists, they are seldom actually read or seriously studied. Cultural patterns make Western military pedagogies more predisposed to follow the precepts of Clausewitz which align best with their history.

Sun Pin, a Chinese commander and military writer who lived some twenty-three centuries ago, said, "However mighty the state, whoever takes pleasure in war will perish." It is also true that, "though war may take place only once in a hundred years, it must be prepared for it as if it could break out the very next day."[92] Chinese military texts attributed to Sun Tzu emphasise the radical and effective nature of deception in Chinese warfare. Warfare as a way of deception favours an unchoreographed, asymmetric approach to fighting while rejecting any notion of constancy in warfare.[93]

"Those who can win a war well can rarely make a good peace and those who could make a good peace would never have won the war"[94] is paradoxically contradictory. "Wars are never won but always lost."[95] Therefore, the point of interpreting the main goals of the war as the implementation of the state's policy goes far beyond just winning the single battle. The balance of world powers nowadays is shaped in a way that makes "big" battles unlikely, because the enemy simply doesn't want to face a stronger opponent in the open field.

There is no panacea for peace that can be written out in a formula. But one can set down a series of practical points – elementary principles drawn from the sum of human experience in all times. Study war, and learn from its history. Keep strong if possible. In any case, be cool. Have unlimited patience. Never corner an opponent, and always assist him to save face. Put yourself in his shoes – so as to see things through his eyes. Avoid self-righteousness and two commonly fatal delusions – the idea of victory and the idea that war cannot be limited. These points were all made, explicitly or implicitly, by Sun Tzu and Kautilya.

It should not be surprising that the Eastern view war is different than the West. Any student of war who has read Sun Tzu, Kautilya or Clausewitz can attest to that. Two main themes dominated ancient Chinese military strategic thought. One was the idea that power dwelt among the people—*Shih*. The other was the strategic principle that the essence of military art lay in deceiving the enemy—intent-based operations. Understanding how your opponent's view of history shapes its world view certainly helps mitigate the chances for strategic miscalculation.

As China's influence on international affairs has continued to grow, more and more people have become concerned about the intentions behind Chinese actions. Several theories offer potential insights into the reasons behind Chinese actions in places like the South China Sea. *Shih* is one of those concepts. *Shih* is a holistic idea that refers to the advantage gained from manipulation of context. Four characteristics help determine whether or not *shih* was a factor in a given conflict. These include leaders seeking to manipulate context, build troop morale through context, use an indirect approach, and exploit propensity within a given situation. Additionally, *shih* provides a contextual approach to operational design.

The global interconnectivity of the 21st century makes interaction with other cultures gather a great salience. Every culture has developed along different historical paths, and a study of the military thought of other cultures can prove useful to understanding concepts of warfighting. They need to be incorporated into professional military education and strategic planning. The rapid changes of the geopolitical environment and conditions for war should impel military thinkers to rethink the concepts of war, both in general and in particular, according to current conditions.

Warfare remains a function largely of the human mind and heart. Students of the military art would do well to consider ancient theorists when framing their own operational problems and designing approaches to solve them. Warfare has a political, social, and cultural context. The basic nature of warfare is unchanging and the nature of war in the 21st century is the same as it was in earlier history.

In all of its more important, truly defining features, the nature of war is eternal. Above all else, war is an instrument of policy. There is more to war than warfare.

Endnotes

1   See Samuel P. Huntington, *The Clash of Civilizations and the Remaking of World Order* (New Delhi: Viking Penguin India, 1996)

2   Victor David Hanson, *Why the West Won: Carnage and Culture: Landmark Battles in the Rise of Western Power* (2nd ed., 2007) pp.147–48.

3   John Keegan, *A History of Warfare* (New York, 2004) p. 387

4   Thomas Rid, "Review of Patrick Porter's Military Orientalism: Eastern War Through Western Eyes." *Journal of Strategic Studies*, 33: 5, (2010) pp. 784-787.

5   *Ibid.*

6   See Patrick Porter, *Military Orientalism: Eastern War through Western Eyes* (London: Hurst & Co., 2009)

7   Patrick Porter, "Good Anthropology, Bad History: The Cultural Turn in Studying War". *Parameters*, (Summer 2007) pp. 45-58.

8   See John Keegan, *A History of Warfare* (London: Pimlico, 1994). It is a wide-ranging survey of the history of war with a focus on the influence of culture on war making. It is a sophisticated attempt to establish a "Western" versus and "Eastern" culture of war, both of which derived from specific historical developments. It has been heavily criticized for both inaccuracies and oversimplification.

9   John Keegan, "In this War of Civilizations, the West will Prevail." *Daily Telegraph*, 8 October 2001.

10 Carl Von Clausewitz, *On War*, Michael Howard and Peter Paret, eds and tr. (Princeton, NJ: Princeton University Press, 1976) pp. 183–4

11   Edward N. Luttwak, *The Grand Strategy of the Roman Empire: From the First Century A.D. to the Third* (Baltimore: Johns Hopkins University Press, 1976) p. xiii

12 Patrick Porter, "Good Anthropology, Bad History: The Cultural Turn in Studying War". *Parameters*, (Summer 2007) pp. 45-58.

13 Peter Paret, The History of War and the New Military History," in *Understanding War: Essays on Clausewitz and the History of Military Power*, ed. (Princeton: Princeton University Press, 1992) pp. 209–26

14   David A. Charters, M. Milner, and J. B. Wilson ed. *Military History and the Military Profession* (Westport: Greenwood Publishing Group, 1992) p.39.

15   Timothy May, *The Mongol Art of War: Chinggis Khan and the Mongol Military System* (Yardley, Pa.: Westholme Publishing, 2007) pp.141–42.

16   Carl von Clausewitz, *On War*, Michael Howard and Peter Paret, eds. and trans. (Princeton, NJ: Princeton University Press, 1976) Antoine Henri de Jomini, *The Art of War* (London, UK: Greenhill Books, 1992)

17   Sun Tzu, *The Art of War*, Samuel B. Griffith, trans. (London: Oxford University Press, 1963)

18   Kautilya, *The Arthaśāstra*, L. N. Rangarajan, ed. and trans. (New Delhi: Penguin Books, 1987)

19   Miyamoto Musashi, *The Book of Five Rings*, Victor Harris, trans. (Woodstock, NY: Overlook Press, 1974)

20   Benjamin R. Maitre, "Echoes and Origins of an American Way of War," *Comparative Strategy*, Vol. 27, No. 3, May/June 2008, pp. 249-251.

21   See Ralph D. Sawyer, *The Seven Military Classics of Ancient China* (New York: Basic Books, 1993)

22   Martin van Creveld, *The Transformation of War* (New York: The Free Press, 1991) p.126

23   Martin van Creveld, *The Culture of War* (New York: Ballantine Books, 2008) p. 257.

24   B. H. Liddell Hart, Foreword to Samuel B. Griffith's trans. Sun Tzu's *The Art of War* (Oxford: University Press, 1963) p. vii

25   Ralph D. Sawyer, *The Complete Art of War* (New York: Westview Press, 1996) p.14

26   Ralph D. Sawyer, *The Seven Military Classics of Ancient China* (New York: Basic Books, 2007) pp. 50–151

27   Sawyer, p. 150.

28   *Ibid.,* p. 63.

29   Sun Tzu, *The Art of War* Chapter 3.18: Attack by Stratagem (Oxford: University Press, 1963)

30   Sun Tzu, p. 77.

31   *Ibid.*, p. 106.

32   *Ibid.*, p. 102.

33   J. Boone Bartholomees, "Sun Tzu and the Art of Modern Warfare," *Parameters*, Vol. 32, No. 3, Autumn 2002, pp. 146-148.

34   Robert L. Cantrell, *Understanding Sun Tzu on the Art of War* (Arlington Virginia: Center for Advantage, 2003) p.60

35   See Col Qiao Li and and Col Wang Xiangsui, *Unrestricted Warfare: China's master plan to destroy America* (Dehradun: Natraj Publishers, 2007)

36   See Col Harjeet Singh, *The Thirty-Six Stratagems* (New Delhi: Pentagon Press, 2014)

37   See Shou Xiaosong, *Science of Military Strategy*, 3rd edition (Beijing: Academy of Military Science Press, 2013)

38   See Sarvepalli Radhakrishnan and Charles A. Moore (eds.) *A Sourcebook in Indian Philosophy* (Princeton: Princeton University Press, 1957)

39   I. W. Mabbett, "The Date of the *Arthasastra*," Journal of the American Oriental Society, 84:2 (April 1965): 162-169.

40   Some Indian scholars trace the origins of the Mahabharata as far back as 1,500 years ago.

41   Roger Boesche, "Kautilya's Arthaśāstra on War and Diplomacy in Ancient India," *Journal of Military History*, Vol. 67, No. 1, January 2003, pp. 9-37

42   *Ibid.* p.19

43   See Chanakya's *Arthashastra* and its Relevance in Modern Warfare. *Trishul* Vol XVIII No.2. Spring 2006. p.81.

44   George J Gilboy, Eric Heginbotham, *Chinese and Indian Strategic Behavior: Growing Power and Alarm* (New Delhi: Cambridge University Press, 2012) p.30

45 *Ibid.*, pp. 236-238.

46 R.P. Kangle, Kautilya *Arthashastra*, Part III, A Study (Bombay: University of Bombay, 1965) Kangle's work is highly recommended. See Book 6 Chapter 2 Sections13-14, 30-38; Book 7 Chapter 1 Sections 2-37; Book 7 Chapter 2 Sections 1-5}.

47 *Ibid.* Book 12 Chapter 1 Sections 1-9; Book 7 Chapter 2 Sections 1-2 and Chapter 5 Sections 13-20

48 *Ibid.* Book 2 Chapter 1 Section 16; Book 7 Chapter 5 Section 27

49   Ibid. Book 7 Chapter 3 Section 12; Book 7 Chapter 5 Sections 16-18; Book 11 Chapter 1 Section 56; Book 13 Chapter 5 Section 3-15

50 *Ibid*

51 Shekhar Adhikari and Sanjeev Bhadauria (Eds.); *India's National Security in the 21ˢᵗ Century* (New Delhi: Pentagon Press, 2014) p. 448

52 Lalit Kumar Das, "Culture as the Designer," *Design Issues*, Vol. 21, No. 4, Autumn 2005, pp. 41-53

53 Rashed Uz Zamam, "Kautilya: The Indian Strategic Thinker and Indian Strategic Culture," *Comparative Strategy*, Vol. 25, No. 3, January-March 2009, pp. 66-88

54 Max Weber, "Politics as a Vocation," in W. G. Runciman, ed., and Eric Matthews, trans., *Weber: Selections in Translation* (Cambridge, UK: Cambridge University Press, 1978) p. 220

55 Uz Raman, p. 235

56 Amrita Narlikar, "Peculiar Chauvinism or Strategic Calculation? Explaining the Negotiating Strategy of a Rising India," *International Affairs*, Vol. 82, No. 11, January 2006, pp. 59-76

57 Thomas Cleary, *The Japanese Art of War: Understanding the Culture and Strategy* (Boston: Shambhala Publications, 1991) p.3

58 *Ibid.* p.4

59 The word *samurai* originally meant "one who serves," and referred to men of noble birth assigned to guard members of the Imperial Court.

60 *Ibid.* p.6

61 *Ibid.*

62 See Miyamoto Musashi, *The Book of Five Rings* trans, Thomas Cleary (Boston: Shambhala Publications, 1993)

63 *Ibid.* p.21

64 *Ibid.*

65 Miyamoto Musashi, *The Book of Five Rings* (trans.) Thomas Cleary (Boston: Shambhala Publications, 2005) p. 53

66 *Ibid.*

67 *Ibid.,* p. 59

68 *Ibid.,* p. 56

69 *Ibid.,* p. 45

70 *Ibid.,* p. 46

71 *Ibid.,* p. 49

72 Benjamin R. Maitre, "Echoes and Origins of an American Way of War," *Comparative Strategy*, Vol. 27, No. 3, May/June 2008, pp. 248-266

73 Musashi, p. 49

74 *Ibid.,* p. 80

75 Musashi, p.xxiii

76 Martin van Creveld, *The Culture of War* (New York: Ballantine Books, 2008) p. 213

77 Arabic word meaning "community". It is distinguished from *Sha'b* which means a nation with common ancestry or geography. It can be said to be a supra-national community with a common history.

78 Brig SK Malik, *The Qur'anic Concept of War* (New Delhi: Adam Publishers, 2008) p.142

79 Majid Khadduri, *War and Peace in the Law of Islam* (Baltimore, Md.: John Hopkins Press, 1955), p. 64.

80 *Ibid.*

81 *Ibid.,* p. 57

82   Ibid.

83   Ibid., p. 58.

84   *Ibid.* p.143

85   *Ibid.* p.144

86   *Ibid.* p.145

87   *Ibid.*

88   John Keegan, "In this War of Civilizations, the West will Prevail." *Daily Telegraph*, 8 October 2001.

89   *Ibid.*

90   Rudolph Peters, *Jihad in Classical and Modern Islam* (Princeton, N.J.: Markus Weiner Publishers, 1996), pp. 44-51, 128.

91   J. Boone Bartholomees, *U.S. Army War College Guide to National Security Issues: Theory of War and Strategy* Vol I, https://publications.armywarcollege.edu/pubs/2182.pdf p. 148.

92   RD Sawyer (ed)., *Military Methods* (Boulder, CO: Westview Press, 1995) p.84

93   Ren Li, *Lectures on Sunzi's Art of War* (Beijing: PLA Press, 2013) p.32 6. Ren Tingguang and Li Weiguo, *Sun Tzu's Art of War: Collected Expositions* (Beijing: PLA Press, 2013), pp. 27-28.

94   Ian Bickerton, *The Illusion of Victory: The True Costs of Modern War* (Melbourne: Melbourne University Press 2011) p.1

95   Karl R. Popper, *Objective Knowledge: An Evolutionary Approach* (Oxford: Clarendon Press, 1972) p.81

BIBLIOGRAPHY

Books

1. Antoine Henri de Jomini, *The Art of War* (London, UK: Greenhill Books, 1992)

2. Carl Von Clausewitz, *On War*, Michael Howard and Peter Paret, eds and tr. (Princeton, NJ: Princeton University Press, 1976)

3. Brig SK Malik, *The Qur'anic Concept of War* (New Delhi: Adam Publishers, 2008)

5. Col Harjeet Singh, *The Thirty-Six Stratagems* (New Delhi: Pentagon Press, 2014)

5. Col Qiao Li and Col Wang Xiangsui, *Unrestricted Warfare: China's master plan to destroy America* (Dehradun: Natraj Publishers, 2007)

6. David A. Charters, M. Milner, and J. B. Wilson ed. *Military History and the Military Profession* (Westport: Greenwood Publishing Group, 1992)

7. Edward N. Luttwak, *The Grand Strategy of the Roman Empire: From the First Century A.D. to the Third* (Baltimore: Johns Hopkins University Press, 1976)

8. George J Gilboy, Eric Heginbotham, *Chinese and Indian Strategic Behavior: Growing Power and Alarm* (New Delhi: Cambridge University Press, 2012)

9. Ian Bickerton, *The Illusion of Victory: The True Costs of*

Modern War (Melbourne: Melbourne University Press 2011)

10. J. Boone Bartholomees, *U.S. Army War College Guide To National Security Issues: Theory Of War And Strategy* Vol I, https://publications.armywarcollege.edu/pubs/2182. pdf

11. John Keegan, *A History of Warfare A History of Warfare* (London: Pimlico, 1994)

12. Karl R. Popper, *Objective Knowledge: An Evolutionary Approach* (Oxford: Clarendon Press, 1972)

13. Kautilya, *The Arthaśāstra*, L. N. Rangarajan, ed. and trans. (New Delhi: Penguin Books, 1987)

14. Majid Khadduri, *War and Peace in the Law of Islam* (Baltimore, Md.: John Hopkins Press, 1955)

15. Martin van Creveld, *The Transformation of War* (New York: The Free Press, 1991)

16. Martin van Creveld, *The Culture of War* (New York: Ballantine Books, 2008)

17. Max Weber, "Politics as a Vocation," in W. G. Runciman, ed., and Eric Matthews, trans., Weber: *Selections in Translation* (Cambridge, UK: Cambridge University Press, 1978

18. Miyamoto Musashi, *The Book of Five Rings*, Victor Harris, trans. (Woodstock, NY: Overlook Press, 1974)

19. Miyamoto Musashi, *The Book of Five Rings* trans, Thomas Cleary (Boston: Shambhala Publications, 1993)

20. Patrick Porter, *Military Orientalism: Eastern War through Western Eyes* (London: Hurst & Co., 2009)

21. Peter Paret, The History of War and the New Military

History," in *Understanding War: Essays on Clausewitz and the History of Military Power*, ed. (Princeton: Princeton University Press, 1992)

22. Samuel P. Huntington, *The Clash of Civilisations and the Remaking of World Order* (New Delhi: Viking Penguin India, 1996)

23. RD Sawyer (ed), *Military Methods* (Boulder, CO: Westview Press, 1995)

24. RP Kangle, *Kautilya Arthashastra, Part III*, A Study (Bombay: University of Bombay, 1965)

25. Ren Li, *Lectures on Sunzi's Art of War* (Beijing: PLA Press, 2013)

26. Ren Tingguang and Li Weiguo, *Sun Tzu's Art of War: Collected Expositions* (Beijing: PLA Press, 2013)

27. Ralph D. Sawyer, *The Seven Military Classics of Ancient China* (New York: Basic Books, 1993)

28. Ralph D. Sawyer, *The Complete Art of War* (New York: Westview Press, 1996)

29. Robert L. Cantrell, *Understanding Sun Tzu on the Art of War* (Arlington Virginia: Center for Advantage, 2003)

30. Rudolph Peters, *Jihad in Classical and Modern Islam* (Princeton, N.J.: Markus Weiner Publishers, 1996)

31. Sarvepalli Radhakrishnan and Charles A. Moore (eds.) *A Sourcebook in Indian Philosophy* (Princeton: Princeton University Press, 1957)

32. Shekhar Adhikari and Sanjeev Bhadauria (Eds.); *India's National Security in the 21st Century* (New Delhi: Pentagon Press, 2014)

33. Shou Xiaosong, *Science of Military Strategy*, 3rd edition

(Beijing: Academy of Military Science Press, 2013

34. Sun Tzu, *The Art of War*, Samuel B. Griffith, trans. (London: Oxford University Press, 1963)

35. Thomas Rid, "Review of Patrick Porter's Military Orientalism: Eastern War Through Western Eyes." *Journal of Strategic Studies*, 33: 5, (2010)

36. Thomas Cleary, *The Japanese Art of War: Understanding the Culture and Strategy* (Boston: Shambhala Publications, 1991)

37. Timothy May, *The Mongol Art of War: Chinggis Khan and the Mongol Military System* (Yardley, Pa.: Westholme Publishing, 2007)

38. Victor David Hanson, *Why the West Won: Carnage and Culture: Landmark Battles in the Rise of Western Power* (2nd ed., 2007)

Journals/Newspapers

1. Amrita Narlikar, "Peculiar Chauvinism or Strategic Calculation? Explaining the Negotiating Strategy of a Rising India," *International Affairs*, Vol. 82, No. 11, January 2006

2. Benjamin R. Maitre, "Echoes and Origins of an American Way of War," *Comparative Strategy*, Vol. 27, No. 3, May/June 2008, pp. 248-266

3. John Keegan, "In this War of Civilizations, the West will Prevail", *Daily Telegraph*, 8 October 2001

4. Patrick Porter, "Good Anthropology, Bad History: The Cultural Turn in Studying War". *Parameters*, (Summer 2007)

5. Benjamin R. Maitre, "Echoes and Origins of an American

Way of War," *Comparative Strategy*, Vol. 27, No. 3, May/June 2008

6. I. W. Mabbett, "The Date of the Arthasastra", *Journal of the American Oriental Society*, 84:2 (April 1965)

7. J. Boone Bartholomees, "Sun Tzu and the Art of Modern Warfare", *Parameters*, Vol. 32, No. 3, Autumn 2002

8. Lalit Kumar Das, "Culture as the Designer," *Design Issues*, Vol. 21, No. 4, Autumn 2005

9. Rashed Uz Zamam, "Kautilya: The Indian Strategic Thinker and Indian Strategic Culture," *Comparative Strategy*, Vol. 25, No. 3, January-March 2009

10. Roger Boesche, "Kautilya's Arthaśāstra on War and Diplomacy in Ancient India," *Journal of Military History*, Vol. 67, No. 1, January 2003

About the Author

Colonel Harjeet Singh (Retd) was commissioned into the Sikh Light Infantry in 1969 and took early retirement in 1998. He holds a MSc and MPhil in Defence and Strategic Studies from University of Madras. A keen student of military history, he is the author of many articles and monographs on defence and strategic affairs. He has over a dozen published books to his credit and is well-known for his erudition and perspicacity of analysis.

www.ingramcontent.com/pod-product-compliance
Lightning Source LLC
Chambersburg PA
CBHW071248130726
47998CB00003B/1102